QUEEN'S

FIND OUT ABOUT

the
body

Anita Ganeri

BBC

© **Anita Ganeri / BBC Education 1994**

BBC Education
201 Wood Lane
London W12 7TS

ISBN 0 563 35543 3

Editor: Christina Digby
Designer: Claire Robertson
Picture research: Helen Taylor
Series consultant: Mary Hoffman
Educational adviser: Su Hurrell
Photographer: Lesley Howling
Illustrator: Aziz Khan

With grateful thanks to:
Kyle Green, Chatelle-Marie Aujla, Ross Williams,
Lily Bateman, Kathryn Earl, Jack Hobbs,
Alasdair Meldrum, Paul Ellaby, Luke Finn,
Terry Mulholland, Gloria Howling

Printed in Belgium by Proost

Contents

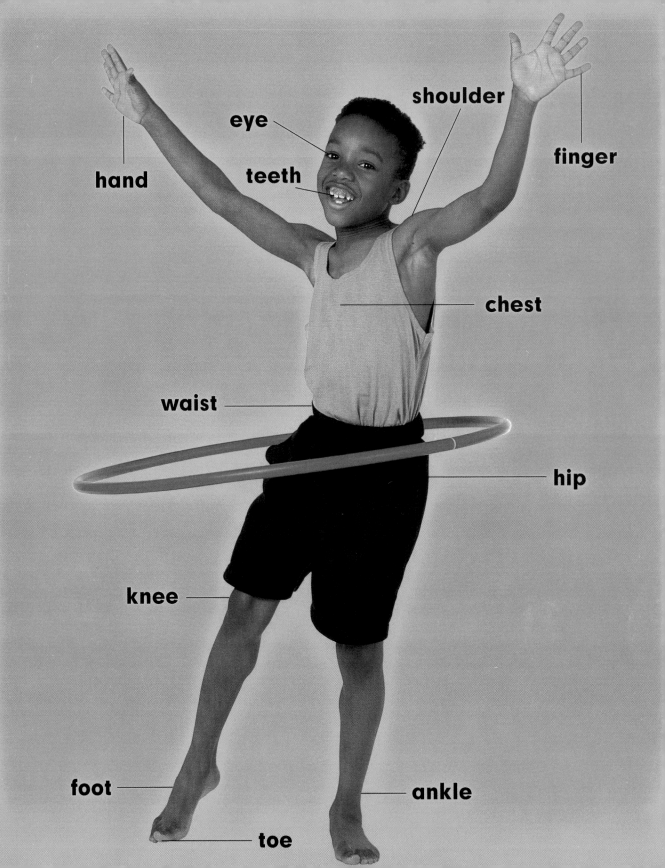

Look at me!

What can you see when you look in the mirror? You see your body! Can you point to your eyes, your knees, your teeth and your toes?

Everyone is made the same way but we all look different. Are you tall or short? Are your eyes brown or blue? Is your hair curly or straight?

All these things make you special.

Look closely at your hands, and think about all the useful things they can do. You can use them to . . .

lift a glass

hold sweets

grip a pencil

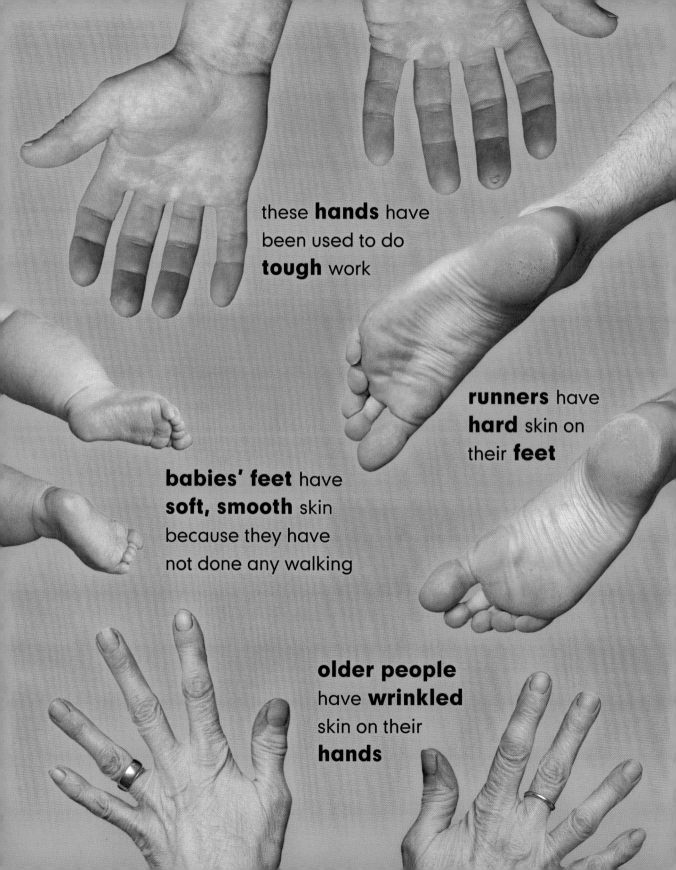

these **hands** have been used to do **tough** work

runners have **hard** skin on their **feet**

babies' feet have **soft, smooth** skin because they have not done any walking

older people have **wrinkled** skin on their **hands**

What's on the outside?

Your whole body is covered in skin. There is skin on your arms and your legs, on the soles of your feet, even on your eyelids. Skin can be different colours from pale pink to dark brown. What colour is your skin?

Skin is soft and stretchy. It lets you bend, twist, frown and smile. It is tough and waterproof and protects your body from harm.

Most of your skin is covered in hair. When you are cold, the hair on your arms stands up to keep you warm. You get bumps on your skin called goose pimples. When you are hot, sweat trickles from your skin. It cools you down.

You might see **goose pimples** on your **arm**.

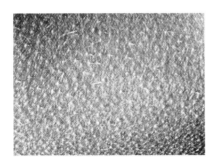

You might see drops of **sweat** on your **forehead**.

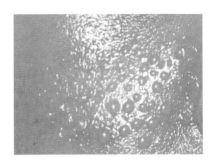

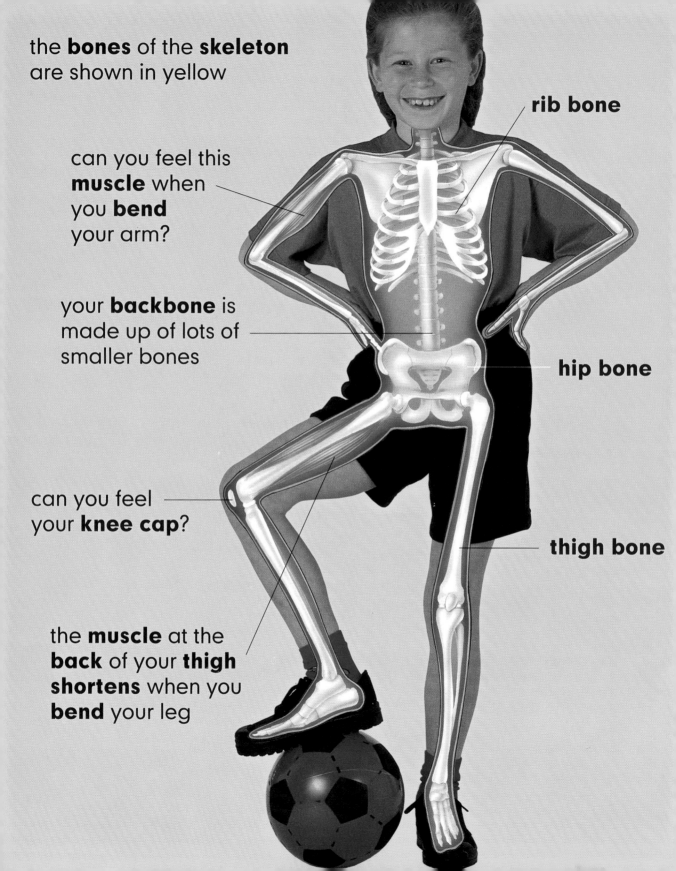

the **bones** of the **skeleton** are shown in yellow

rib bone

can you feel this **muscle** when you **bend** your arm?

your **backbone** is made up of lots of smaller bones

hip bone

can you feel your **knee cap**?

thigh bone

the **muscle** at the **back** of your **thigh** **shortens** when you **bend** your leg

How do we move?

Can you feel hard, knobbly things under your skin? These are your bones. They are strong and hard and hold up your body. You have lots of bones, joined together to make up your skeleton. Without bones, you would flop like jelly.

Rubbery muscles are attached to your bones. Your bones and muscles work together when you move. You use your muscles when you walk, talk, run or play games.

Can you feel the muscles in your arms and legs?

You also use **muscles** to smile and make faces.

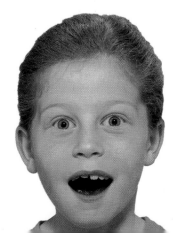

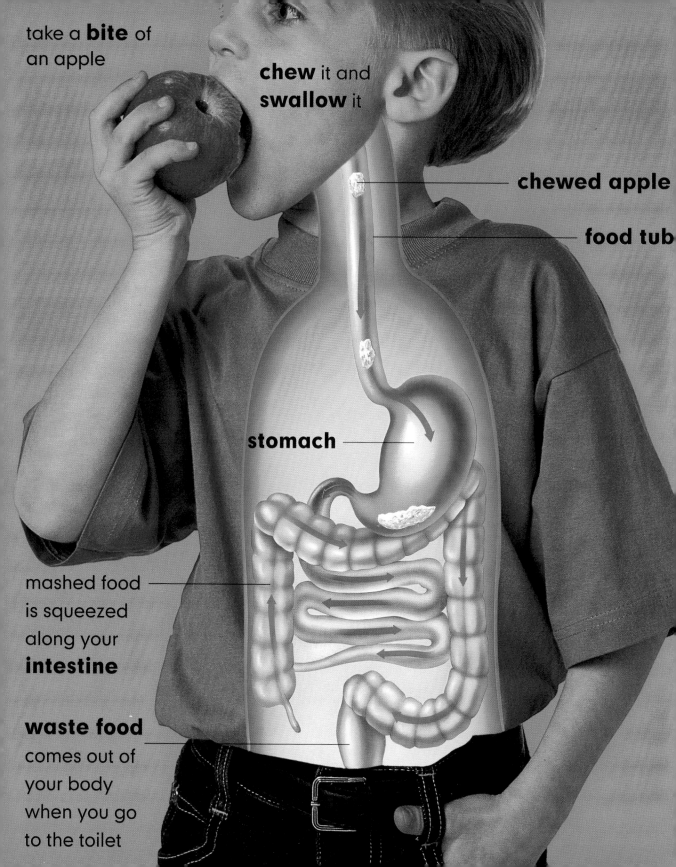

take a **bite** of an apple

chew it and **swallow** it

chewed apple

food tube

stomach

mashed food is squeezed along your **intestine**

waste food comes out of your body when you go to the toilet

Where does food go?

When you eat a bite of an apple, where does it go? First your teeth bite and chew the apple so it is easy to swallow. Then it goes down a tube into your stomach. It is mashed some more. It is squeezed down a very long tube, called your intestine. Useful parts of the food are used by your body. They give you energy and help you grow. Waste food comes out of your body when you go to the toilet.

To stay healthy, you need to eat different types of food.

Some foods help you **grow**.

Some foods give you **energy**.

Some foods keep your **teeth**, **skin** and **bones** healthy.

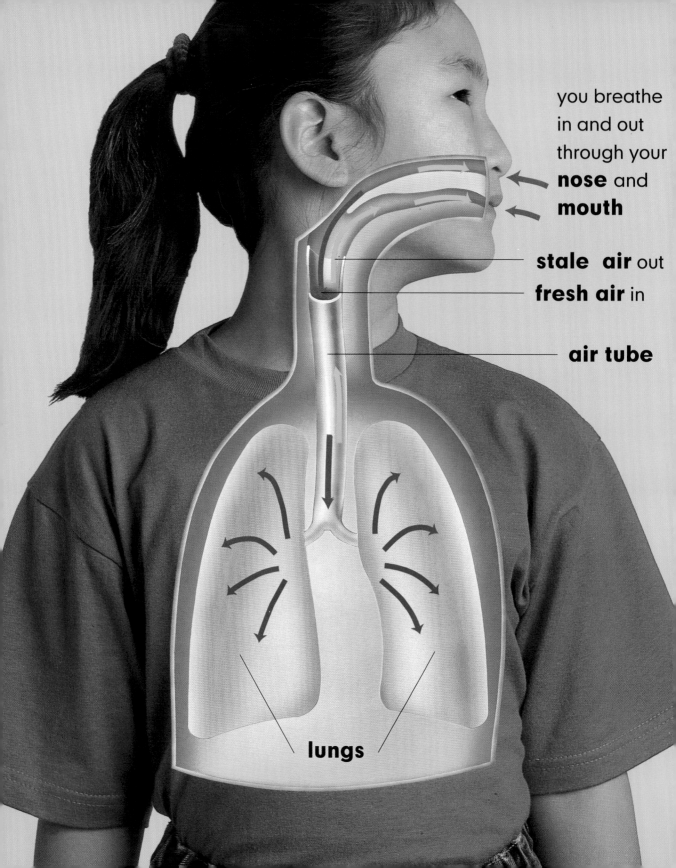

you breathe
in and out
through your
nose and
mouth

stale air out

fresh air in

air tube

lungs

How do we breathe?

You breathe all the time, even when you are asleep.

When you breathe in, you suck fresh air in through your nose or mouth. It goes down the air tube in your throat, then into two spongy bags in your chest. These are your lungs.

As you breathe in your chest gets bigger to give your lungs room to fill with fresh air.

As you breathe out your chest gets smaller to squeeze stale air out of your lungs and back out through your nose and mouth.

breathing **in** fresh air

breathing **out** stale air

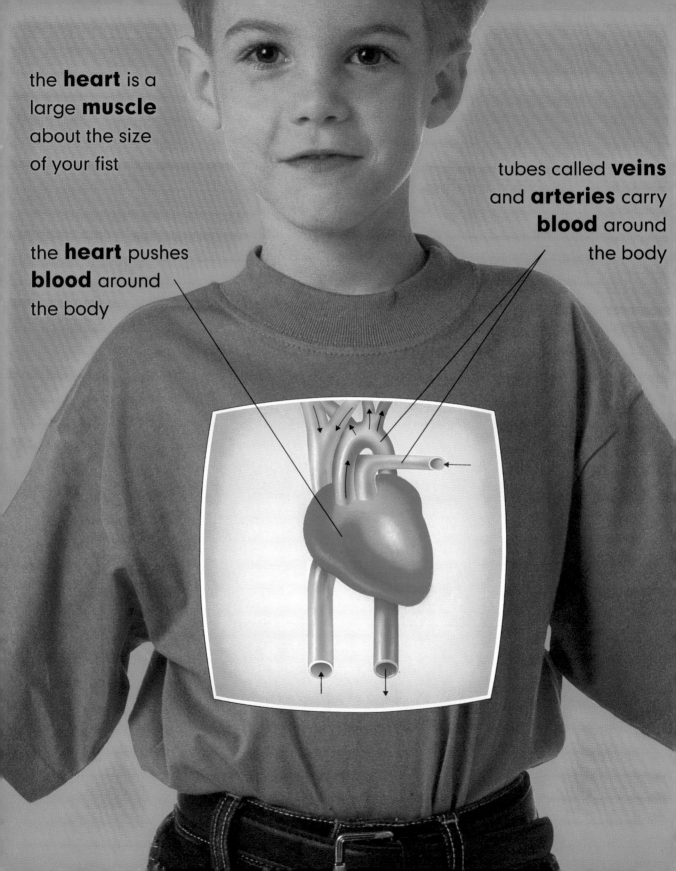

the **heart** is a large **muscle** about the size of your fist

the **heart** pushes **blood** around the body

tubes called **veins** and **arteries** carry **blood** around the body

What is blood?

If you cut or graze yourself, you see blood coming out. Blood flows round and round your body through tiny tubes. Blood never stops moving. This is because your heart is a big strong muscle which keeps pushing blood through the tubes.

Blood has an important job to do. It carries the useful things found in food and air to all the parts of your body.

Blood moves faster around your body when you move faster.

If you graze your knee, **blood** comes out of the wound.	Soon the **blood** forms a **scab** to cover the cut while it heals.

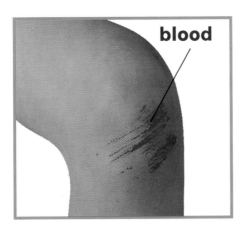

blood

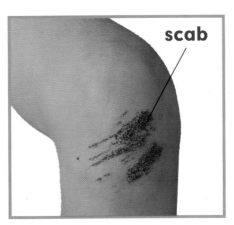

scab

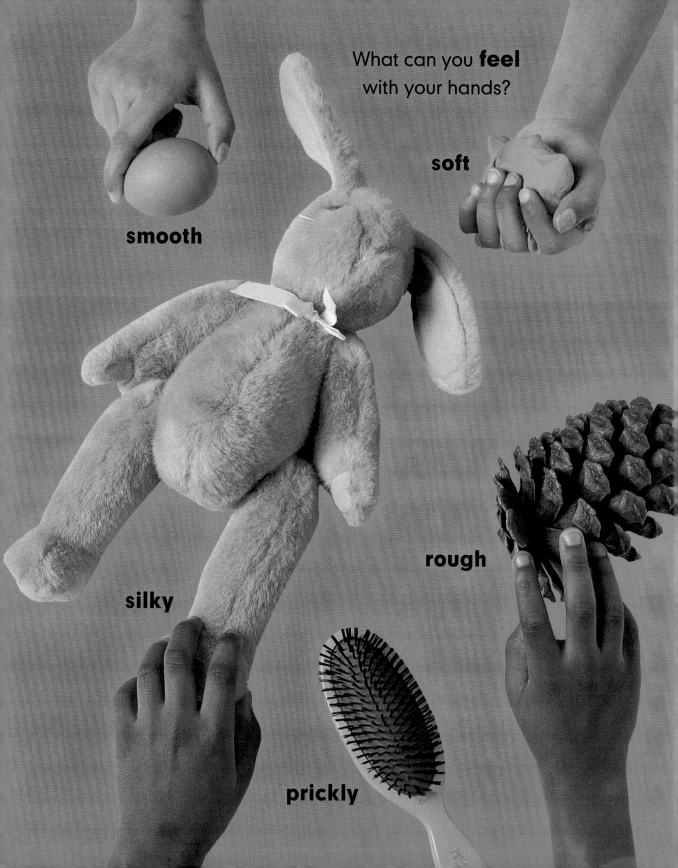

What can you **feel** with your hands?

smooth

soft

silky

rough

prickly

What can you feel?

You have five senses which tell you about the world around you. These are touch, sight, hearing, taste and smell.

You touch and feel things with your skin. It tells you if things are soft or hard, rough or smooth, hot or cold. A furry toy feels soft and silky. A pine cone feels hard and rough. The skin on your fingers is very good at feeling things.

Some blind people can read special books. They use their sense of touch to read tiny bumps with their fingertips.

This pattern of bumps is called **Braille**.

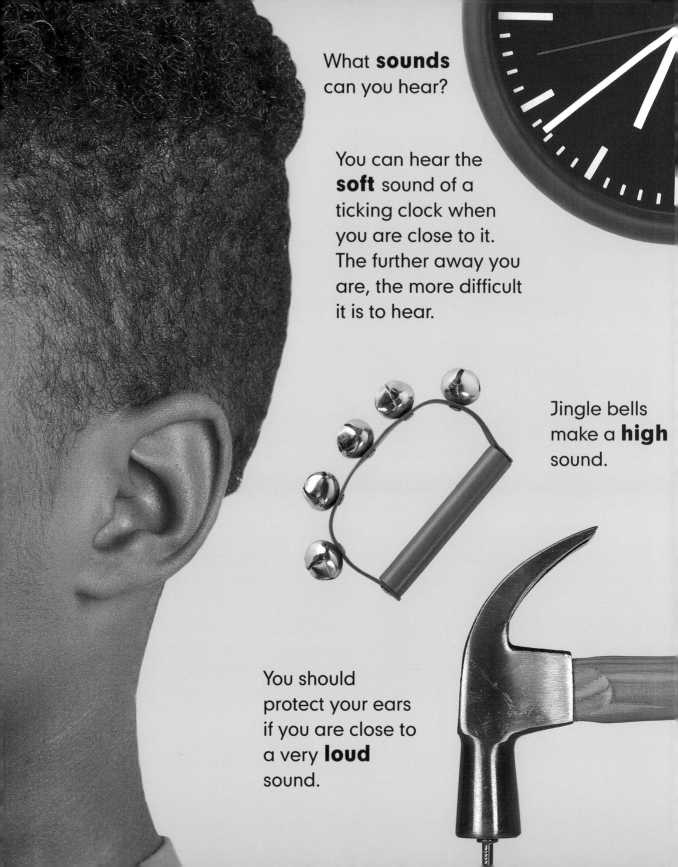

What **sounds** can you hear?

You can hear the **soft** sound of a ticking clock when you are close to it. The further away you are, the more difficult it is to hear.

Jingle bells make a **high** sound.

You should protect your ears if you are close to a very **loud** sound.

What are eyes and ears for?

You see with your eyes and hear with your ears. You can hear different sounds, loud and soft. You can only see part of your ear. The rest of your ear is hidden deep inside your head.

Your eyes send information to your brain to tell you what things look like, their colour, shape and size. The black dot in the middle of your eye is really a tiny hole called the pupil. This is what you see through.

Eyes can be different colours. What colour are your eyes?

You might want to wear **sunglasses** to protect your eyes in bright sunshine. What difference does this make to what you see?

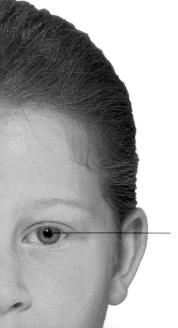

— **pupil**

Which things taste
sweet, salty, sour, bitter?
Which are **warm** and **cold**?

What can you taste and smell?

You use your tongue to taste your food and drink, and to find out if it is hot cold. Your tongue also tells you about flavours. We all like different flavours. Some things are sour like cooking apples or salty like tears. Others are bitter like coffee or sweet like honey.

You smell things with your nose. Your senses of taste and smell work together. If your nose is blocked, you can't taste your food properly.

We like some smells more than others.

food gives you **energy**, keeps you **healthy** and helps you **grow**

exercise can be fun

washing keeps you **clean**

How do we stay healthy?

You need to look after your body. This means eating healthy food, taking regular exercise and getting plenty of rest. Exercise is good for keeping your heart, lungs and muscles healthy. It can also be fun!

Don't eat too many sweets, biscuits or crisps. They are bad for your teeth. Munch on an apple or pear instead.

Don't forget to keep clean too!

A good night's sleep gives your body a chance to recover from its busy day.

Index